Autumn Peltier, Water Warrior

Written by
Carole Lindstrom

Illustrated by
Bridget George

Roaring Brook Press

New York

For water warriors everywhere, aaniin*. The earth and I embrace you. xx —C. L.

*I see the light in you.

For Noah—my Little Thunderer—and all the children of the seventh generation:
May you be always be as powerful and as gentle as water. Gizaagi'in*. —B. G.

*I love you.

Published by Roaring Brook Press
Roaring Brook Press is a division of Holtzbrinck Publishing Holdings Limited Partnership
120 Broadway, New York, NY 10271 · mackids.com

Photo credits: 36: © Ayşe Gürsöz; 38: (top) © Linda Roy, (bottom) © UN Photo/Manuel Elías

Our books may be purchased in bulk for promotional, educational, or business use. Please contact your local bookseller
or the Macmillan Corporate and Premium Sales Department at (800) 221-7945 ext. 5442 or
by email at MacmillanSpecialMarkets@macmillan.com.

Library of Congress Control Number: 2022920583

First edition, 2023

Book design by Aram Kim and Mercedes Padró

Printed in China by Toppan Leefung Printing Ltd., Dongguan City, Guangdong Province

ISBN 978-1-250-79527-4

1   3   5   7   9   10   8   6   4   2

❧ Foreword by Autumn Peltier ❧

My relationship with water and my work as an Indigenous water advocate and an Indigenous Rights Activist began with my late Aunt Josephine. This celebration of her work, her guidance, and her legacy brought me to tears. I could feel her spirit as I read—as I took in the words and illustrations that depicted our water journey so well—and it felt like she was smiling. In our culture, we look at water as a living being, and we're taught to treat it with the same respect we would show another human. Water is the lifeblood of Mother Earth. It gives all life, and there is no life without it.

My hope is that young people learn from our story and use their voices to speak up for future generations!

—Autumn Peltier, Indigenous Rights Activist,
2023, Ontario, Canada

I am nibi.
I have a spirit.
I have feelings.
I remember.

For a very long time,
all life on Earth cared for me.
Looking seven generations into the future
to make sure I was pure and clean—
for their children's children.

I remember . . .
how the Anishinaabe
cherished me,
loved me.

Speak for the water.

Sing for the water.

Dance for the water.

Over time, more people came.

Diminishing their voices.

Drowning out their message.

Those people didn't care for me.

Didn't cherish me.

Didn't love me.

As my voice grew quieter,

the women who cared for me

were forced to get louder.

And then I met Grandma Josephine.

I remember her touch.

The ripple.

She walked miles and miles around the Great Lakes,
carrying my spirit in her copper pail
so people would see her.
And see me.

The seventh generation is creating
a sea of change.

It was a soft voice at first.
Like a ripple.
But with practice, it grew louder.

When Grandma Josephine
journeyed on to the spirit world,
Autumn, her great-niece,
began to use her voice for me.

Autumn is the seventh generation.
She honors me through ceremony,
offering up asemaa and prayers
for my health and well-being.
I know Autumn, and Autumn knows me.

Speak for the water.

Sing for the water.

Dance for the water.

When she saw signs that read:
STOP! WATER NOT SAFE
to drink,
to wash,
to touch . . .

She summoned her courage
and confronted the people who made decisions.
Telling them she was unhappy with their choices.

Telling them that I am precious.

Telling them that without me, there would be no life.

There would be nothing.

Her ancestors knew that as the seventh generation,
Autumn would one day raise her voice.

Though she began in her great-aunt's footsteps,
Autumn is blazing her own path.

For me.

Speak for the water.

Sing for the water.

Dance for the water.

For the next seven generations.
For healthy animals
and plants,
for you,
for me.

With Grandma Josephine guiding her,
and the women who came before her,
Autumn visited different Indigenous communities.
She met leaders from all over the world.

Speaking out,

loud and strong,
for me.

Like a ripple in a vast sea,
people are beginning to wake up and listen.
But I need all of you now.
To grow the ripple into a
tidal wave.

Be like Autumn
and Grandma Josephine,
leave good footprints,
for me.

Speak for the water.

Sing for the water.

Dance for the water.

What will you do for me?

JOSEPHINE HENRIETTA MANDAMIN, WATER WALKER

*Water is very precious, and I will go to any lengths
and direction to carry the water to the people.*
—Josephine Mandamin

Josephine Henrietta Mandamin, or Grandmother Josephine, as she was lovingly known, was a respected Anishinaabe Elder and an internationally recognized water and Indigenous rights activist. She was widely acknowledged as the leader of the Water Walk movement, mentoring young generations of water warriors like her great-niece Autumn Peltier.

In 2003, Josephine cofounded the Mother Earth Water Walkers. Comprised of women from different clans, Mother Earth Water Walkers is an Anishinaabekweg-led organization that draws attention to the water crises in its communities and around the world by walking the perimeter of the Great Lakes.

In the spring of 2003, when Josephine was sixty-one, the Mother Earth Water Walkers held their inaugural Water Walk. They walked the entire circumference of Lake Superior, a distance of 2,726 miles, while carrying a ceremonial copper pail filled with lake water. What Josephine saw while they walked reinforced their mission: "The heaviness in our hearts was unbearable when we saw the destruction of the forests, the Earth being gouged by machines, the rivers and creeks dying in the human filth amid green slime and brown, poison fluid flowing into the cleaner rivers."

Their walk around Lake Superior took a total of 35 days to complete and launched the Water Walk movement as we know it today. Speaking for the water is considered a matriarchal act; women lead the ceremony while men walk beside them, carrying an eagle staff.

Between 2003 and 2017, Josephine and the Mother Earth Water Walkers conducted a total of thirteen Water Walks, walking over 15,000 miles to advocate for the importance of clean water. That distance is more than half the Earth's circumference and equates to approximately 250 days of continuous walking. After her first Water Walk in 2003, Josephine wrote, "When the walk got tiring and painful, this was ever on my mind: The next generation will remember the Water Walk, our grandchildren will remember the Water Walk, and so on to the next generations. Not one of us was separate. We walked as one."

These are lessons she passed on to her great-niece Autumn Peltier and water activists everywhere. As the world faces an impending climate crisis, Indigenous peoples play a critical role in preventing ecological destruction and climate catastrophe.

The United Nation's top climate change body, the Intergovernmental Panel on Climate Change, says without justice for Indigenous people, climate change will certainly get worse. But in too many conversations about these issues, many tribes like Josephine's are not invited to the table.

Grandmother Josephine passed away on February 22, 2019, at the age of seventy-seven.

AUTUMN PELTIER, WATER WARRIOR

Autumn Peltier is Anishinaabe and an Indigenous Water Protector from Wiikwemkoong First Nation on Manitoulin Island in northern Ontario.

In 2012, at the age of eight, Autumn discovered that many First Nations Communities in Ontario were on boil-water advisories—some for several years—and she began speaking out about the importance of water on her reserve. She knew that clean water should be a right for all.

In 2016, at the age of twelve, Autumn first captured the media's attention when she confronted Canada's Prime Minister, Justin Trudeau, at the winter meeting of the Assembly of First Nations. In front of thousands, she bravely told the Prime Minister he wasn't doing enough to protect their country's water.

In July 2017, Autumn received the Governor General of Canada Sovereign's Medal for Volunteers, which recognizes exceptional volunteer achievements of Canadians from across the country in a wide range of fields.

In 2018, she addressed the United Nations General Assembly in New York.

In 2019, at the age of fourteen, Autumn was appointed Chief Water Commissioner for the Anishinaabek Nation, a position previously held by her great-aunt Josephine Mandamin. In her role, Autumn meets with leaders from different Tribal Nations, speaks nationally and internationally about Indigenous rights and water rights, and is instrumental in protecting the water that leads in and out of the Great Lakes. She has been nominated several times for the International Children's Peace Prize.

Also in 2019, Autumn spoke at the Global Landscapes Forum, the world's largest knowledge-led platform on integrated land use. The forum takes a holistic approach to create sustainable landscapes that are productive, prosperous, equitable, and resilient. It is led by the Center for International Forestry Research, in collaboration with its cofounders, the United Nations Environment Programme, the World Bank, and Charter Members.

The work Autumn is doing today—work she began hand-in-hand with her great-aunt Josephine—is turning the water warrior message into a tidal wave of change. However, Autumn acknowledges there is still much work to be done.

There are a lot of youth that are standing up, and it's because we're really
seeing the effects of climate change. A lot of us youth are scared. We are wondering,
do we even have a future to look forward to?
—Autumn Peltier

With more voices like Autumn's and YOURS, we can all work together to address the climate crisis!

GLOSSARY

Anishinaabekweg—Anishinaabe women. In Anishinaabe culture, women have always been the water protectors of the community.

asemaa—tobacco (Anishinaabe). The Anishinaabe people use tobacco as an offering in ceremony. It is offered to nibi with a prayer for nibi's health and out of respect.

nibi—water (Anishinaabe).

seven generations—Anishinaabe people believe that when a decision is made, it must be based on how it will affect the next seven generations. Consideration must always be given to how actions today impact those who will come after.

KEEP LEARNING

We are guided by visions and dreams, but most of all we are guided by our Spirit
and Spirit Helpers. The journey with the water has become a lifetime experience,
in that, the work is year-round. More women and young girls are hungering for
women's teachings. We must feed their hunger.
—Josephine Mandamin, 2005 Lake Huron Water Walk

Every year, Grandmother Josephine and the Mother Earth Water Walkers documented their historic journey around the Great Lakes. You can read their journals, learn more about their movement, and view photos of their Water Walks at MotherEarthWaterWalk.com.

In 2020, fifteen-year-old Autumn Peltier was featured in a documentary called *The Water Walker* produced by Seeing Red 6Nations, an Indigenous-owned media company based on Six Nations of the Grand River Territory. The powerful short film follows Autumn as she prepares to speak in front of the United Nations—detailing her passion, dedication, and profound commitment to advocate for clean water for Indigenous communities around the world.

My Aunt Josephine, she inspired people globally, raising awareness and
praying for the water. Her dying wish was for me to carry on her work.
—Autumn Peltier, The Water Walker

KEEP READING

Nibi Emosaawdang / The Water Walker, written and illustrated by Joanne Robertson; translated by Shirley Williams and Isadore Toulouse

Young Water Protectors: A Story About Standing Rock by Aslan Tudor and co-writer Kelly Tudor